10/2005

J
92
RICE

Wade, Mary Dodson.

Condoleezza Rice.

$17.85   stacks   P

10/03/2005

DATE		
NOV 30 05		
APR 03 09		

WITHDRAWN

CONDOLEEZZA RICE

CONDOLEEZZA RICE

Being the Best

MARY DODSON WADE

A Gateway Biography
The Millbrook Press
Brookfield, Connecticut

Published by The Millbrook Press, Inc.
2 Old New Milford Road
Brookfield, Connecticut 06804
www.millbrookpress.com

Library of Congress Cataloging-in-Publication Data
Wade, Mary Dodson.
Condoleezza Rice : being the best / Mary Dodson Wade.
p. cm. — (A gateway biography)
Summary: Introduces National Security Advisor, Condoleezza Rice, from
her childhood in Birmingham, Alabama, to her amazing scholarly and
musical accomplishments and involvement in foreign affairs.
Includes bibliographical references and index.
ISBN 0-7613-2619-7 (lib. bdg.)
ISBN 0-7613-1927-1 (pbk.)
1. Rice, Condoleezza, 1954—-Juvenile literature. 2. National Security
Council (U.S.)—Biography—Juvenile literature. [1. Rice, Condoleezza,
1954- 2. National Security Council (U.S.)—Biography. 3. Women—
Biography. 4. African Americans—Biography.] I. Title. II. Series.
UA23.15 .W343 2003
355'.03307'092—dc21 2002003412

Cover photograph courtesy of © Getty Images/Shawn Thew

Photographs courtesy of AP/Wide World Photos: pp. 3, 6, 30, 34, 38;
Birmingham Public Library Archives: p. 9 (Catalog #29-3-4-25-8);
University of Denver, Special Collections: pp. 11, 18, 20, 22; Getty
Images: pp. 15 (© Otillie Johnson), 33 (© Chris Hondros/Newsmakers),
36 (© Larry Downing/Reuters), 37 (© Reuters), 40 (© Larry Downing/
Reuters); George Bush Presidential Library: pp. 24, 26; Hoover
Institution Archives: p. 28

CONDOLEEZZA RICE

National security adviser Condoleezza Rice at a briefing in the White House on September 19, 2001

Growing Up

Nine-year-old Condoleezza Rice stood outside the gate of the White House in Washington, D.C. She stared at the beautiful place where American presidents live. "One day I'll be in that house," she said.

That was a very big dream for the little girl who lived in Birmingham, Alabama. The year was 1963. Segregation kept white and black people apart. There were no white students in her school. Only black people lived in her neighborhood. Public buildings had separate drinking fountains for African Americans. Her family could not even eat at the restaurants in their hometown.

Thirty-seven years later, Condoleezza Rice had a sunny corner office in the White House. It was just a few doors down the hall from the office of President George W. Bush. As national security adviser, she kept the president informed about events that were happening around the world.

Condoleezza's great-great-grandparents had been slaves. When Condoleezza first saw the White House, slavery had been against the law for nearly a hundred years. Still, many African Americans were very poor. As a young man, her grandfather, John Rice Sr., paid rent on the farm where he raised cotton. But he had a dream. He wanted to go to college.

Stillman College in Tuscaloosa, Alabama, was just fifty miles away. It was one of the few places he was allowed to attend. He saved money until he had enough to enroll. His

Condoleezza Rice's friends call her Condi.

money soon ran out, but he did not want to leave. Then he learned that students who were studying to be Presbyterian ministers did not have to pay. John Rice Sr. became a Presbyterian preacher. After graduating he went to Birmingham, Alabama, where he founded Westminster Presbyterian Church.

His son, John Rice Jr., also graduated from Stillman. He was a minister like his father, but he worked as a counselor at a Birmingham high school. When his father retired, John Jr. became pastor of the church but still worked at the school.

John Rice Jr. married a talented musician named Angelena Ray. Her father had never had an opportunity to

Westminster Presbyterian Church, where Condoleezza's father was the pastor. Condoleezza spent a lot of time at the church in children's clubs and youth groups.

go to college, but he made sure that all five of his children did. Angelena taught biology at the high school where John Rice Jr. worked. She also played the organ for services at Westminster Presbyterian.

John and Angelena's daughter was born on November 14, 1954. Her mother named her Condoleezza. The name comes from the Italian musical phrase *con dolcezza*, which means "with sweetness."

The Rice family lived in a part of Birmingham called Titusville. It was a middle-class African-American neighborhood. Many residents owned their own homes. Some were teachers like Condoleezza's parents. Others were preachers and shop owners. There was even a doctor.

Activities in the community centered around the church. People attended services every Sunday. Condoleezza was part of the church's children's clubs. Later, she joined the youth fellowships.

Her father worked especially hard to help the young people. The burly pastor coached after-school sports and led trips to the art museum. He provided tutors for students who needed extra help with schoolwork. He organized clubs to teach chess and Ping-Pong. He even taught the students how to waltz and on weekends held dances for them. Growing up in this tightly knit community gave Condoleezza a great sense of security.

She was about four years old the first time she saw a white person. It was Christmastime, and her parents took her to see Santa Claus. She sat on his lap, staring at the man in the red suit.

As she grew, Condoleezza's parents gave their bright little girl every opportunity to develop her talents. She had

John W. Rice Jr. was Condoleezza's father. He and her mother encouraged her to get a good education and work hard to make the most of her talents and abilities.

her mother's musical ability. She began piano lessons when she was three years old. She could read music before she could read words. At the age of four she gave her first piano recital.

Her father called her "Little Star." He loved to tell about the time when an older, five-year-old child had the lead part in a talent program. Condoleezza thought she should have been given the part. During the performance, the star suddenly got stage fright. Condoleezza pushed aside the tongue-tied child and sang the song herself.

Mrs. Rice kept close watch on her daughter. She bought all of Condoleezza's Girl Scout cookies rather than let her child go door-to-door to sell them. She shopped at the best department stores. The dressing rooms were only for white people, but she refused to buy anything unless the clerk let Condoleezza try on the dresses.

At the age of five, Condoleezza was ready to start school, but her November birthday meant that she would have to wait. Her mother stayed home from work that year and taught her. Condoleezza entered public school in the second grade, skipping the first grade. Later, she skipped seventh grade as well.

Her father believed that education was a person's best defense. He always said, "If it's in your head, no one can take it away from you." Her parents enrolled Condoleezza in many book clubs. Books began to stack up beside her bed. Often textbooks given to schools with minority children were old and outdated. The Rices bought new textbooks for Condoleezza's class so that they could study current information.

Condoleezza's after-school hours were filled with activities. She learned to ice skate. She took ballet lessons. Three times a week she studied French. She continued piano lessons, and became so skilled that she was allowed to take lessons at the all-white Birmingham Southern Conservatory of Music.

She did well in everything. Her parents built her self-confidence even more by including her in family decisions. She got to choose dinner menus and help decide about family outings. Their strong support and encouragement convinced Condoleezza that she could be anything she wanted to be, even president of the United States.

Years later, a confident Condoleezza Rice remembered those early years. "You were taught that you were good enough, but you might have to be twice as good, given you're black."

Parents in the Titusville section of Birmingham knew that their children would face racism. They protected the children from it as much as they could. Many never rode public transportation, where they would have to sit at the back of the bus. But it was hard to hide the fact that the city swimming pools were for white children only. Minority children were allowed into Kiddieland amusement park only one day a year. Condoleezza ignored Kiddieland. Instead, she went to Coney Island, a much bigger park, while her father was studying at Columbia University in New York City.

A Time of Change

Condoleezza was about nine when two things happened that made her aware of the struggle for equality. Dr. Martin Luther King Jr. was leading peaceful protest marches in the South. When the marchers came to Birmingham, the Rices did not join them. Condoleezza's father felt that education was the way to overcome segregation, but he wanted his daughter to understand what was happening.

With Condoleezza up on his shoulders, he stood some distance away. Police arrested so many marchers that the state fairgrounds was the only place large enough to hold them. Condoleezza went with her father to check on some of his students who were there.

Then, on September 15, 1963, a hate group called the Ku Klux Klan exploded a bomb in the Sixteenth Street

Condoleezza grew up in Birmingham, Alabama, where, in 1963, Dr. Martin Luther King Jr. and other civil rights leaders led peaceful protest marches to encourage an end to segregation.

Baptist Church. Condoleezza's church was a few miles away, but she heard the blast that Sunday morning. Four young girls were killed. One of them was Denise McNair. Condoleezza had attended birthday parties with Denise.

There were more bombings, but the police did nothing. Condoleezza's father joined other men to patrol the neighborhood at night to keep their families safe.

Often during the summers, the family traveled to different colleges while John Rice worked on higher education degrees. When Condoleezza was eleven, they moved to Tuscaloosa, Alabama. For the next two years, her father served as dean of Stillman College.

At thirteen, Condoleezza was very happy to learn that they were moving to Colorado. Her father had finished his studies at the University of Denver and was made vice chancellor of the school. Living in Denver meant that she could ice-skate year-round.

She entered tenth grade at St. Mary's Academy and immediately faced some surprises. At the all-girls school, she had to wear a uniform. And, for the first time, she had white classmates.

School had always been easy for Condoleezza. This was no different. She raced through courses. By the time her senior year came, she already had enough credits to graduate. She was only fifteen years old. Even so, a counselor at the school did not think that she, a black student, should try to go to college.

In the Rice family the question was not whether to attend college, but when. Her parents wanted her to enroll at the University of Denver right away. Condoleezza disagreed. She felt that everyone should finish high school. She solved the problem by doing both. Every day she got up at 4:30 A.M. and raced off to ice-skate. Then she went to the university and took two classes. In the afternoon she returned to St. Mary's.

By midterm, high school did not seem nearly so interesting, but she completed the year at St. Mary's. Her date for the senior prom was a college hockey player.

For years, she had spent hours playing classical music by Mozart, Brahms, and Beethoven. No one was surprised when Condoleezza announced that she was going to be a concert pianist. Her proud parents gave her a beautiful Steinway grand piano.

Even though Condoleezza loves to play classical music, she often listens to Led Zeppelin's rock music as she works out each day.

Several months later she mentioned that she wanted to attend the famous Juilliard School of Music in New York City. Her father cautioned against it. "You might change your mind." She did not believe that could possibly happen.

Condoleezza at the University of Denver

She never went to Julliard because, halfway through college, she did change her mind. She had always been the best at everything she did. She did not want to be anything less than the best concert pianist. "Mozart didn't have to practice. I was going to have to practice and practice and practice and was never going to be extraordinary."

Her other choices as a music major were to teach piano students or to play for singers. She did not want to do either. She left the music department.

Condoleezza had trouble finding a new subject that interested her. Then, one evening, she went to a lecture that set the direction of her life.

Choosing a Path

Professor Josef Korbel had been an ambassador in his native Czechoslovakia. He had fled the country to escape the Nazis during World War II. Eventually he came to the United States. When Communists took over his homeland, he became a fiercely loyal American citizen.

Professor Korbel was head of the Department of International Relations at the University of

Josef Korbel's daughter, Madeleine Albright, became Secretary of State during President Bill Clinton's term. She moved out of her White House office at the time Condoleezza Rice moved into hers.

Josef Korbel in 1976, a few years after Condoleezza heard his lecture about Joseph Stalin and international relations with the Soviet Union, which had a big effect on her career in politics

Denver. Condoleezza heard his lecture on Soviet dictator Joseph Stalin. She knew immediately that she wanted to study the way countries developed and interacted with each other.

In his lectures, Professor Korbel showed how politics affected the way governments responded in times of crisis. She was fascinated. The professor became a powerful influence in her life, second only to her parents. "I adored him," she said. "He is the reason I am in this field."

She chose to study the Soviet Union. She had always liked Russian music and culture. She had read Russian authors. Now she studied the history and politics of the giant Communist country. She learned to speak perfect Russian.

Condoleezza has a deep religious faith and attends church almost every Sunday. Among her favorite hymns are "I Need Thee Every Hour" and "His Eye Is on the Sparrow."

Professor Korbel was impressed with his pupil. She visited his home often. They enjoyed lively political discussions.

Condoleezza was only nineteen years old when she graduated from the University of Denver. Her degree was given "with honors." She was a member of Phi Beta Kappa, the honor society.

The following year she was at Notre Dame University in South Bend, Indiana, earning a Master of Arts degree

Condoleezza joined the faculty at Stanford University after earning her doctorate in political science from the University of Denver.

in political science. Then she returned to the University of Denver to study with her favorite teacher. Unfortunately, Josef Korbel did not live to see her complete her Ph.D. degree several years later.

After receiving her degree, the twenty-seven-year-old graduate was ready for even more intense study. She left Colorado snows for sunny California. She went to study military arms control at Stanford University in Palo Alto.

After she had been there a few months, she gave a lecture. The teachers were so impressed that they asked her to join the political science department. The young black woman took her place among older, white men, but no one questioned her knowledge of international affairs.

The classes Condoleezza taught were very popular. Often she set up mock national crises. Students had to work out ways to respond in order to save the country. These methods earned her a teaching award.

International Politics

During the time Condoleezza was teaching at Stanford, General Brent Scowcroft came to the campus as a guest speaker. Young Professor Rice asked some hard questions. Scowcroft was impressed. "Here was this slip of a girl. She wasn't cowed by the company she was in. And she made sense."

In 1988, when George Bush became president, he chose General Scowcroft as his national security adviser. The general immediately telephoned Condoleezza Rice. He invited her to come to Washington to be his adviser on Soviet affairs.

She was in her mid-thirties and was again surrounded by gray-haired men. These men in military uniforms listened to information provided by the Soviet expert. President George Bush introduced her to Soviet President Mikhail Gorbachev by saying, "This is Condoleezza Rice. She tells me everything I know about the Soviet Union."

In her new job she traveled with the president when he went overseas. In Russia, she set up a series of classes. The *Moscow Times* was totally surprised. Condoleezza did not talk about cooking. She talked about missiles.

Tiny, always well dressed, she charmed everyone with her smile and polite manners. Fellow workers, however, discovered that she could be tough as steel. When Russian President Boris Yeltsin came to Washington in 1989, he

Condoleezza with Mikhail Gorbachev in 1990, the same year he won the Nobel Peace Prize for his work toward world peace

insisted that he must see the president. Condoleezza stood in the doorway, blocking the world leader, who was almost twice her size. In perfect Russian, she told him that his interview was with General Scowcroft. After five minutes, President Yeltsin gave up and met with the national security adviser.

While Condoleezza was serving in Washington, incredible events changed the world. Poland broke away from Communism. The Soviet Union split into separate countries. The ugly concrete wall in Germany that separated Communist East Berlin from free West Berlin was torn down. Condoleezza made many trips to Germany to help reunite that country.

Provost of Stanford

In 1991, Condoleezza was ready to return to California. She wanted a quieter life. She was tired of having to deal with international crises at any hour of the day or night. She returned to Stanford to teach. In 1992 she earned the Dean's Award for Distinguished Teaching from the School of Humanities and Sciences.

The following year the thirty-eight-year-old professor was named provost of the university. She ranked second

President George H.W. Bush and Condoleezza speaking together in the White House in 1991 before she left Washington to return to Stanford University

only to the president of the school. This surprised many people. Every other Stanford provost had been at least sixty years of age. No woman, and certainly no African American, had ever been provost of the university.

Critics complained that she had no experience for this job. Condoleezza saw it as a challenge. "I love this university, and I thought I had a chance to do something good for it."

Some people believed that she got the Stanford job because of her race. She made clear her belief that any person hired for a job should be qualified to do it. "I've always felt you should not see race and gender in everything. You should give people the benefit of the doubt." Her success soon quieted the critics, but there was trouble at first.

As provost, she controlled the money that paid the teachers and provided student services. She faced a huge problem. The previous Stanford president had spent large sums of money on expensive things. The school was $43 million in debt.

She slashed budgets and fired teachers. Professors were angry because they had not been asked to help make decisions. Then she did away with the job held by a popular Hispanic administrator. Mexican-American students staged sit-ins and hunger strikes.

Typically, she did not let the protests bother her. She had studied the problem and worked out a solution. She did what she thought best. To her, worrying over things in the past is useless. She summed the situation up with her favorite phrase, "Get over it. Move on."

While provost of Stanford University, Condoleezza met Volker Ruehe (second from left), German minister of defense, in 1995.

Her plan worked. Stanford no longer had debts. Even those who had complained admitted that the university was better because of what she did. She proudly keeps a paperweight saying that Stanford met its budget during the six years she was provost.

She did more than balance budgets, though. Music was still a large part of her life. Her piano was her treasure. Each time she moved, she picked the apartment by first judging where she could put the piano. In Palo Alto, she played twice a week with a chamber-music group. Occasionally she gave concerts on campus.

The little girl whose father had taught her to love football also turned into a huge sports fan. She had season passes to Stanford ball games, and even traveled to other cities to cheer for the team. For her forty-fourth birthday, she spent the whole weekend going to a women's basketball tournament, a football game, and a men's basketball game. After that she watched the San Francisco 49ers on television. A friend remarked, "She'll watch anything with a score at the end."

Football is a special passion. She has been a Broncos fan since the time she lived in Denver. If a Broncos game was not on TV, she telephoned a friend in the place where the game was being played and listened to the play-by-play over the phone. She joked, "I probably would have written more books if I didn't watch NFL Sunday."

Because her parents had provided opportunities for her, Condoleezza tried to do the same for others. After her mother died in 1985, her father moved to California. Condoleezza and her father started an after-school academy in a poor section of East Palo Alto. The Center for a New Generation serves students in grades two through eight. Every day tutoring and music lessons are offered. Extra help is given to students who want to go to college.

Condoleezza has said that she would like some day to be football commissioner. Friends think she would be good at that. They have also suggested that George W. Bush, who used to own the Texas Rangers, would make a good baseball commissioner someday.

As Stanford provost from 1993 to 1999, Condoleezza was a huge fan of the Stanford University football team, coached by Tyrone Willingham, shown here with Condoleezza in October 2000.

The Center stresses positive attitudes. Condoleezza once talked with a girl who was discouraged about her chances to succeed. The girl knew that 65 percent of her classmates never finished high school. Condoleezza said to her, "What makes you think you have to be one of that 65 percent?"

Her important job at Stanford brought many honors. She became a fellow (member) of the American Academy of Arts and Sciences. She served on the board of directors of several companies. She was also on the boards of charities, research organizations, and the National Endowment for the Humanities. But service on these boards ended when she returned to Washington.

Condoleezza had not planned to live on the East Coast when she took a break from Stanford in 1999. Many people assumed that she would become president of another university. She surprised everyone by returning to Russian studies and to her music. In the summer of 2000 she attended a week-long music camp in Montana. She played classical music twelve hours a day.

The Chevron company often names oil tankers for members of their board of directors. Condoleezza had one named for her. The Condoleezza Rice was a supertanker, the largest that would go through the Suez Canal. It had a double hull as protection against oil spills. Several bad spills had hurt the environment, and Condoleezza joked, "When you have a tanker named for you, no news is good news." She is no longer on the board. The tanker was sold and renamed.

Someone asked her if she relaxed by playing music. She responded, "The great thing about playing classical music is that you can't hold anything else in your head . . . it's not relaxing to play Mozart or Brahms; it's challenging. But in its challenge, it takes you into another space, and I love that."

Back in Washington, D.C.

Politics, however, would not go away. While Condoleezza was in Washington the first time, she had developed a warm friendship with President George Bush and his wife, Barbara. Now, ten years later, their son Texas Governor George W. Bush was thinking about running for president. The former president invited Condoleezza to the Bush summer home in Kennebunkport, Maine. That weekend, she met the future president and his wife, Laura.

The three of them became instant friends. They were near the same age. They laughed at the same things. Condoleezza and the governor were both avid sports fans. In between sailing, playing tennis, and working out on the treadmill, the two discussed foreign policy decisions that the next president would face.

Their friendship grew. Condoleezza visited the Texas governor's mansion many times that year. She was invited

At the Republican National Convention in August 2000 Condoleezza spoke in favor of candidate George W. Bush for president.

to go with the Bushes to inspect a ranch in central Texas that they wanted to buy. It was late July and grasshoppers were everywhere. She could not imagine what they liked about the area. "But once we got in the truck and started going down in the canyons I could see why. Now I really love being out there."

One of the things that she liked about George W. Bush was his desire to give everyone a chance to succeed. She

Condoleezza and Paul Wolfowitz, another adviser, with Republican presidential candidate George W. Bush at his Crawford, Texas, ranch in September 2000

remembers the high school counselor who did not think she should go to college. Like her father, she thinks education leads to success. "In America, with education and hard work, it really does not matter where you came from; it matters only where you are going."

During George W. Bush's campaign for president in 2000, she helped him form his foreign policy. She coached him during the presidential debates. Sometimes he strayed off the topic. She warned him to start over and make the statements he wanted to emphasize. She compared it to playing classical music or performing an ice-skating routine. "You can't wing it," she said.

After George W. Bush won the election, most people expected Condoleezza Rice to be named Secretary of State. Instead, the new president chose her as his national security adviser. He knew that she was brilliant and had experience in foreign affairs. He liked her ability to understand and explain complicated situations. "I trust her judgment," he said.

Often she has strong ideas about what should be done, but she must offer other choices as well. "I have to be very disciplined about making sure I'm giving the president the whole picture."

In her new job, she again traveled with the president. One trip took them to Russia to meet President Vladimir

Senior adviser Karl Rove and national security adviser Condoleezza Rice were sworn in on January 22, 2001, one day after President George W. Bush was sworn in as the forty-third president.

Putin. The Russian people loved the fact that she spoke their language so well. The meeting helped establish good relations between the two leaders whose countries had once been enemies.

For almost a year, the new administration worked on programs that would make life better for the citizens of the United States. Then, on September 11, 2001, terrorists crashed planes into buildings in New York City and Washington, D.C. Thousands of Americans died. The nation was stunned by the attack.

As an expert on Russian international relations, Condoleezza met with Russian President Vladimir Putin in July 2001.

The president and his staff focused on how to respond to this threat to the country. The poised, gracious woman who could have been a concert pianist was part of this team directing events that affected the whole world.

The president ordered American planes to strike at terrorist groups hiding in Afghanistan. Afghanistan is a poor country in Asia where people suffered under a harsh government. Years of drought had killed the crops. President

Condoleezza Rice and other members of the National
Security Council met with President George W. Bush
after September 11, 2001. Of the September 11 attacks
Condoleezza said, "It is one of those events that foreign
policy professionals spend their lives talking about and
thinking about and studying . . . but you hope
to God that you'll never actually face it."

Bush wanted to let the Afghan people know that the United States was not at war with them. Condoleezza suggested sending food as a message of peace. Hundreds of thousands of packets of food were dropped from airplanes over northern Afghanistan.

Condoleezza Rice's abilities are impressive. In describing her, the editor of *Foreign Affairs* magazine used a popular saying. "Most people learned in the affairs of state can't screw in a lightbulb, and most people who can screw in a lightbulb can't restore American authority in the world. She can do both."

Some people have called her a role model for girls and minorities. She brushes that aside. To her, the necessary thing is to set goals and achieve them. "I hear the word 'role model' and I don't mind that, but I'd like to think that I could be a role model for some young white males, too."

John Rice Jr. died in December 2000, right before Condoleezza took her job as national security adviser. But he lived long enough to know that his daughter had made good on her promise to be in the White House.

Those who know her think she may someday hold even higher offices. A Stanford history professor thought that she might become Senator Rice. Another professor was just as sure that she could be the first female president of the United States.

Condoleezza steps off Air Force One
after flying with President Bush to
Charlotte, North Carolina, in April 2001.

Condoleezza Rice concentrates on the job she is doing. "I have learned to do what works for me—and that is not to look that far ahead; to do what you're doing, do it well, and see what comes next."

Important Dates

November 14, 1954	Condoleezza Rice is born in Birmingham, Alabama
1957	Begins piano lessons
September 15, 1963	Bomb kills four young black girls in Birmingham church
1967	Moves to Denver, enters St. Mary's Academy
1970	Takes college courses during her senior year of high school
1972	Meets Josef Korbel, the teacher who most influenced her life
1974	Earns bachelors degree in political science from University of Denver
1975	Earns Master of Arts degree in political science from Notre Dame University
1977	Josef Korbel dies
1981	Earns Ph.D. degree in Soviet politics and culture from University of Denver; studies arms control and disarmament at Stanford University; joins faculty at Stanford
1984	Publishes a book about the Soviet Union and the Czech Army; receives Stanford's Walter J. Gores

	Award for Excellence in Teaching; makes speech that impresses General Brent Scowcroft
1986	Publishes a book about Russian president Mikhail Gorbachev
1988	George H. W. Bush is elected president; Rice is invited to Washington by Brent Scowcroft
1989	Special assistant to President Bush on national security affairs
1990	Becomes senior adviser on Soviet affairs
1991	Returns to Stanford
1993	Appointed as Stanford provost
1995	Publishes a book about Germany becoming one nation again
1998	Invited to Kennebunkport, Maine, to talk with presidential candidate George W. Bush
2000	Advises George W. Bush during presidential campaign
2001	Named national security adviser to President George W. Bush
September 11, 2001	Terrorist attacks on New York City and Washington, D.C.
October 15, 2001	Speaks on Arab language TV network, Al Jazeera, to counter statements of American hatred against Muslims
2002	Accompanies Yo-Yo Ma in a concert at the National Humanities Awards

Further Reading

Bredeson, Carmen. *George W. Bush: The 43rd President*. Berkeley Heights: Enslow, 2002.

Bredeson, Carmen. *Laura Bush: First Lady*. Berkeley Heights: Enslow, 2002.

Reed, Julia. "The President's Prodigy." *Vogue*, October 2001, 396–403ff.

"Rice, Condoleezza," *Current Biography*, April 2001, 74–79.

Russakoff, Dale. "Lessons of Might and Right." *The Washington Post*, September 9, 2001.

Index